OUR
GRE★T
STATES

WHAT'S GREAT ABOUT

UTAH?

✳ Rebecca Felix

LERNER PUBLICATIONS ✳ MINNEAPOLIS

CONTENTS

UTAH
WELCOMES YOU! ✳ 4

Copyright © 2015
by Lerner Publishing Group, Inc.

Content Consultant: Eric G. Swedin, PhD,
Professor of History, Weber State University

Lerner Publications Company
A division of Lerner Publishing Group, Inc.
241 First Avenue North
Minneapolis, MN 55401 USA

For reading levels and more information, look
up this title at www.lernerbooks.com.

Main body text set in ITC Franklin Gothic Std
Book Condensed 12/15.
Typeface provided by Adobe Systems.

Library of Congress Cataloging-in-Publication
Data

Felix, Rebecca, 1984–
      What's great about Utah? / by Rebecca
Felix.
           pages cm.
      Includes index.
      ISBN 978-1-4677-3864-4 (lib. bdg. :
alk. paper) — ISBN 978-1-4677-6088-1
(pbk.) — 978-1-4677-6266-3 (EB pdf)
      1. Utah—Juvenile literature. I. Title.
F826.3.F47 2015
   979.2—dc23   2014031569

Manufactured in the United States of America
1 – PC – 12/31/14

UTAH Welcomes You!

Welcome to Utah, home to many great outdoor adventures! Visitors travel from around the world to ski and snowboard in Utah. See world-class athletes practice for the Olympics in Utah's gorgeous mountains. Other natural beauties in Utah include the Great Salt Lake and red rock canyons. See coyotes, eagles, and hawks in the desert. Join real-life cowboys as they rope cattle and ride horses on ranches. Or maybe you'd like to see the stars at Clark Planetarium. Read on to find out about ten things that make Utah great!

Welcome to UTAH

LIFE ELEVATED

Explore Utah's parks and all the places in between! Just turn the page to find out about the BEEHIVE STATE. >

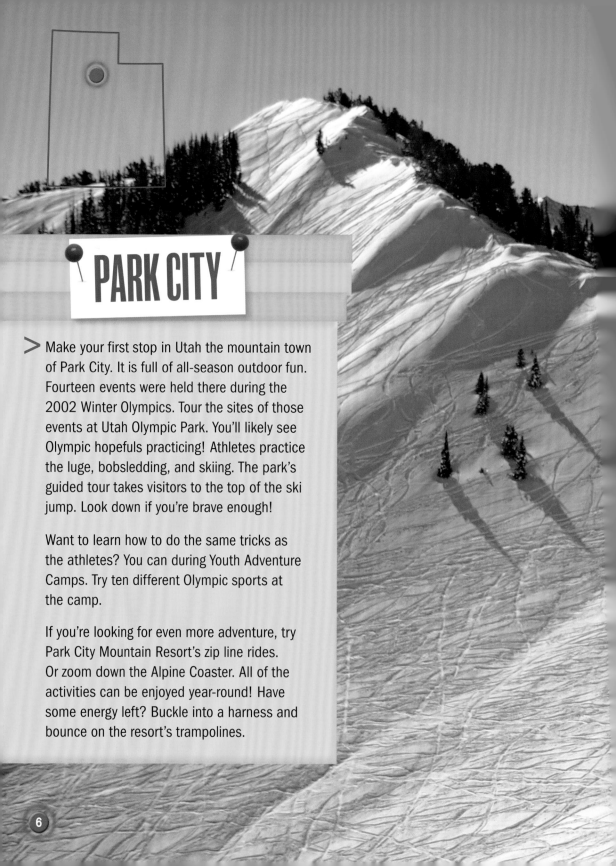

PARK CITY

> Make your first stop in Utah the mountain town of Park City. It is full of all-season outdoor fun. Fourteen events were held there during the 2002 Winter Olympics. Tour the sites of those events at Utah Olympic Park. You'll likely see Olympic hopefuls practicing! Athletes practice the luge, bobsledding, and skiing. The park's guided tour takes visitors to the top of the ski jump. Look down if you're brave enough!

Want to learn how to do the same tricks as the athletes? You can during Youth Adventure Camps. Try ten different Olympic sports at the camp.

If you're looking for even more adventure, try Park City Mountain Resort's zip line rides. Or zoom down the Alpine Coaster. All of the activities can be enjoyed year-round! Have some energy left? Buckle into a harness and bounce on the resort's trampolines.

During the summer, watch athletes at Utah Olympic Park practice launching off a ramp and jumping into the park's huge pool.

While anchored to the trampoline at Park City Mountain Resort, you can flip, jump, and spin!

DINOSAUR PARK

> Imagine walking along a forest trail when you suddenly hear branches snap. A thundering roar rises. You look up to see a dinosaur! But don't worry. It won't hurt you. This is a life-size robotic sculpture. Check out more than one hundred dinosaur statues at Ogden's George S. Eccles Dinosaur Park. Stereos play sounds of dinosaur footsteps and roars.

The sculptures are based on real fossils. Many of the dinosaurs roamed Utah millions of years ago. And many of the museum's fossils come from Utah too! Scientists prepare the fossils for display in the laboratory.

After checking out the displays, go on a fossil hunt. A plastic stegosaurus skeleton is buried outdoors. You can help archaeologists carefully dig up the bones.

UTAH DINOSAURS

Millions of years ago, when dinosaurs were alive, the land in Utah was swampy. The Rocky Mountains formed around this time. As the mountains formed, rock was pushed downhill. The heavy rocks covered dead dinosaurs and plants. The dinosaurs were buried deep under the rock. Pressure and heat turned the dinosaur bones to rock.

You can watch scientists work on fossils at George S. Eccles Dinosaur Park.

ROCKIN' R RANCH

> Don't miss Rockin' R Ranch in Antimony. This ranch has real cowboys to teach you how to rope cattle and ride horses! Start your cowboy adventure on the bucking barrel. This big barrel hangs from ropes. Hold on! Other visitors shake the ropes as you ride. It feels as if you're riding a bucking bronco.

After your ride, have a cowboy teach you to lasso. Learn to brush and feed the horses before exploring mountain trails on a horseback ride. Or if you'd like to relax, sign up for a wagon ride. You'll see all the sights of Antimony from the comfort of a hay bale.

If it's really hot outside, splash in the ranch's swimming pond. Fly into the water off the rope swing! You can also float down the Sevier River on a tube.

Watch cowboys wrangle calves and horses during your stay at Rockin' R Ranch.

Guests at the ranch enjoy an evening of dancing after a large meal.

CLARK PLANETARIUM

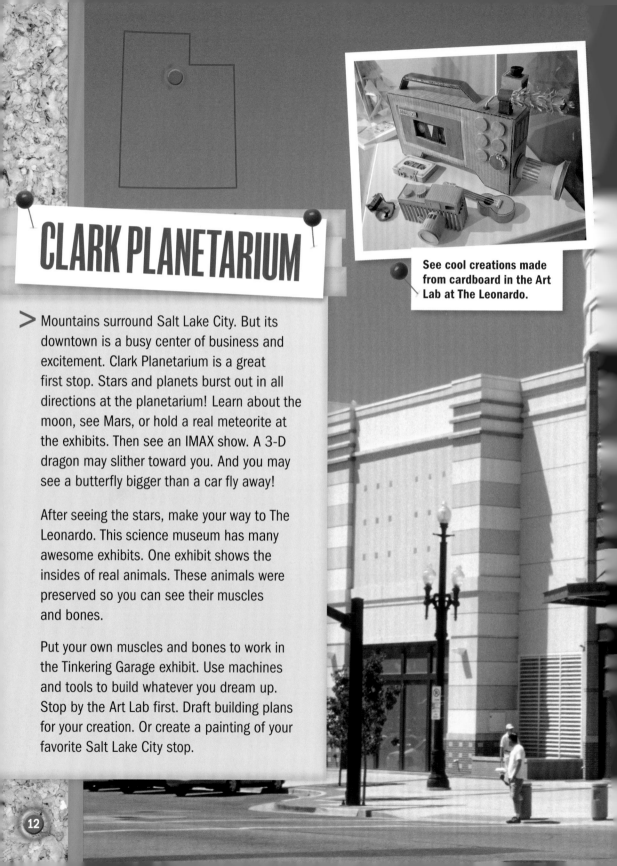

See cool creations made from cardboard in the Art Lab at The Leonardo.

> Mountains surround Salt Lake City. But its downtown is a busy center of business and excitement. Clark Planetarium is a great first stop. Stars and planets burst out in all directions at the planetarium! Learn about the moon, see Mars, or hold a real meteorite at the exhibits. Then see an IMAX show. A 3-D dragon may slither toward you. And you may see a butterfly bigger than a car fly away!

After seeing the stars, make your way to The Leonardo. This science museum has many awesome exhibits. One exhibit shows the insides of real animals. These animals were preserved so you can see their muscles and bones.

Put your own muscles and bones to work in the Tinkering Garage exhibit. Use machines and tools to build whatever you dream up. Stop by the Art Lab first. Draft building plans for your creation. Or create a painting of your favorite Salt Lake City stop.

The IMAX theater screen at Clark Planetarium is five stories tall!

THIS IS THE PLACE HERITAGE PARK

> Continue exploring Salt Lake City at This Is the Place Heritage Park. It has an American Indian village celebrating Utah's native people. Listen to workers in traditional clothing tell stories of the Navajo American Indians' homes.

Stop by the general store in the park's pioneer village. It is stocked with old-fashioned candy and toys. Visit the blacksmith shop next. Watch a costumed worker bend and shape metal using old tools. You can also watch a woodworker carve or see someone spin wool.

If you're at the park during the spring, visit the baby animals. You can hold a tiny chick in your hands. Or you can pet a baby pig, cow, or goat. If you're visiting in the summer, you can see American Indian dancers perform. And be sure to stop by during Pioneer Day in July. Join the watermelon-eating contest. Or test your strength in the giant tug-of-war. Then get ready to catch candy during the parade!

Watch a costumed worker operate a spinning wheel at This Is the Place Heritage Park.

UTAH PIONEERS

Many people who moved to Utah were Mormons. They came to the area looking for freedom to practice their religion. Some walked hundreds of miles to get there. In 1847, Mormon leader Brigham Young came upon what is now Salt Lake City. He famously said, "This is the right place." By the late 1800s, tens of thousands of Mormons had settled in Utah. Mormon pioneers are remembered in Utah on Pioneer Day.

MOAB NATIONAL PARKS

> Moab is a perfect place for an adventure in Utah's desert. The city is home to two of the state's five national parks. Make your first visit Arches National Park. It has more than two thousand natural arches and rock formations. Take a guided hike through mazes of tight canyons at Fiery Furnace.

On the second day of your adventure, take an off-road tour. You can spend a full day exploring Canyonlands National Park. The tour includes stops at ancient American Indian rock drawings and dinosaur tracks in the desert.

If you're looking for a fast-paced activity, sign up for a white-water rafting trip. You can paddle through 14 miles (23 kilometers) of rapids on the Colorado River. Or sign up for a jet boat tour. This guided tour will have you splashing through the rapids. Look up at the towering canyon walls as you zoom by!

The Skyline Arch is one of thousands to see at Arches National Park.

UTAH'S LAND FORMATIONS

Utah has a variety of landscapes. Bonneville Salt Flats are in the northwest. They are miles of hard, flat earth crusted with salt. The flats border the Great Salt Lake. The lake is the largest saltwater lake in the Western Hemisphere. Wetlands also surround the lake. The Wasatch Mountains run from north to south down the middle of the state. They are covered in forests and are part of the Rocky Mountain range. Much of Utah is desert. Southern Utah is a part of the Colorado Plateau.

MILLER MOTORSPORTS PARK

> Motorcycles and off-road buggies ripping up a racetrack are regular sights in Tooele, Utah. Visit Miller Motorsports Park to see these and more high-speed events. Grab some earplugs and get ready for fast, loud fun!

Races are held here throughout the year. Some races take place on dirt. The drivers skid around corners and jump hills. Other races take place on the asphalt track. Some cars go nearly 200 miles (320 km) per hour!

The park hosts go-kart and bicycle races too. Get autographs from the stars after most races. Then hit the track yourself! Kids older than eight years and taller than 51 inches (130 centimeters) can race go-karts.

A professional tests out the dirt track at Miller Motorsports Park.

Race your friends or family on the go-kart track at Miller Motorsports Park.

ANTELOPE ISLAND

> Picture driving 7 miles (11 km) on a causeway into the middle of a lake. You look ahead and see an island! You've arrived at Antelope Island State Park in Great Salt Lake.

Antelope Island is home to many animals, including bison, antelope, bighorn sheep, coyotes, and rabbits. See how many animals you can spot on your visit!

If you're visiting in the warmer months, play on the beach at Bridger Bay. Cool off in the water. You'll float without any effort! It is eight times saltier than the ocean.

After drying off, explore the island. Sign up for a horseback-riding trip. Include a stop at Fielding Garr Ranch. It is a historic, abandoned ranch. Make sure to come back to the ranch for a guided night tour to find out if it is haunted!

WHY IS GREAT SALT LAKE SO SALTY?

Rivers flow into Great Salt Lake. But it does not feed any rivers. This means no water is pushed out from the lake. Water that comes in from rivers has some salt in it. Some of this water evaporates, leaving the salt. Salty water is denser than freshwater. The more salt there is in the water, the denser it is. The water in Great Salt Lake is denser than people—so they float easily!

Bison are just one of the animals you can see on Antelope Island.

POWWOWS AND CELEBRATIONS

> Utah's American Indians host many celebrations each year. They are open to everyone and are a great way to experience the state's cultures.

The Heber Valley Powwow takes place each June. Watch dancers perform in traditional clothing. After watching the dancing, walk through the tents to see jewelry and other treasures for sale. Try traditional dishes of fry bread, roast mutton, or Navajo tacos when you get hungry.

The Utah Navajo Fair is another action-packed celebration. It is held each September in Bluff. The fair begins with a parade and traditional dancing. Drummers compete at a powwow. Try competing in a roping competition on a fake bull. You'll have fun watching the rodeo. Adults and kids compete in many events. Watch cowboys ride bulls and speed through barrel racing courses.

UTAH'S AMERICAN INDIAN NATIONS

There are many American Indian nations in Utah, including Shoshone, Paiute, Ute, Goshute, and Navajo. Utah is named after the Ute nation. The Ute traditionally lived in the eastern and central parts of the state. The Goshute, the Navajo, and the Paiute traditionally lived in Utah's deserts. At powwows, people remember their history and celebrate their culture through dress, songs, and festivities.

The huge feather headdresses sway as the dancers move at the Heber Valley Powwow.

THANKSGIVING POINT

> Thanksgiving Point is a perfect place to finish your tour of Utah. This area in Lehi has a farm, a garden, and a museum complex. Start your day at the Museum of Natural Curiosity. Choose from more than four hundred exhibits. Explore ancient ruins, learn more about the sun and the moon, or perform tricks in the magic shop.

Then make your way to the Museum of Ancient Life. See dinosaur skeletons and ancient sea creatures. On some nights, you can sign up for a late-night museum scavenger hunt. A paleontology class and a 3-D movie follow the hunt. Or enjoy an outdoor movie during the summer on Saturday nights. Lay out your blanket and your movie snacks.

And be sure to check out Farm Country at the park. Sign up to milk a cow. While you wait, pet and feed the sheep, the horses, the pigs, and the llamas. End your stay with a visit to the gardens. Listen for the waterfall as you walk the paths and discover pools, ponds, and a secret garden.

YOUR TOP TEN!

You just read about ten things that make Utah great. What things to do and places to see sounded best to you? What would you include if you were planning a Utah trip? Were there any places or events that weren't in this book? Make a list of your top ten choices. Then turn them into a book just like this one! Draw pictures of the places and activities you chose. Or search the Internet or magazines for images to fill your book. Have fun creating your own Utah top ten list!

You'll see koi fish in the ponds (*left*) and tulips filling the gardens (*right*) during your visit to Thanksgiving Point.

UTAH BY MAP

> ## MAP KEY

⭐ Capital city

○ City

◎ Point of interest

▲ Highest elevation

–·– State border

Visit www.lerneresource.com to learn more about the state flag of Utah.

IDAHO

WYOMING

Great Salt Lake

George S. Eccles Dinosaur Park

WASATCH MOUNTAINS

The Leonardo

Natural History Museum of Utah

This Is the Place Heritage Park

GREAT SALT LAKE DESERT

Ogden

Layton

Antelope Island State Park

UINTA MOUNTAINS

▲ Kings Peak
(13,528 feet/4,123m)

West Valley City

★ **Salt Lake City**

Park City

Park City Mountain Resort

Utah Olympic Park

Miller Motorsports Park
(Tooele)

Sandy

Taylorsville

West Jordan

Orem

Thanksgiving Point
(Lehi)

Provo

NEVADA

COLORADO

Miles

0   20   40   60

0   40   80

Kilometers

N

Sevier River

Green River

Arches National Park

Colorado River

Canyonlands National Park

ESCALANTE

DESERT

Rockin' R Ranch
(Antimony)

Utah Navajo Fair

Glen Canyon National Recreation Area

Glen Canyon

Bluff

St. George

ARIZONA

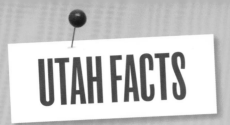

UTAH FACTS

NICKNAME: The Beehive State

SONG: "Utah, This Is the Place" by Sam and Gary Francis

MOTTO: Industry

FLOWER: sego lily

TREE: Colorado blue spruce

BIRD: California gull

ANIMAL: Rocky Mountain elk

DATE AND RANK OF STATEHOOD: January 4, 1896; the 45th state

CAPITAL: Salt Lake City

AREA: 84,897 square miles (219,882 sq. km)

AVERAGE JANUARY TEMPERATURE: 25°F (–4°C)

AVERAGE JULY TEMPERATURE: 73°F (23°C)

POPULATION AND RANK: 2,900,872; 33rd (2013)

MAJOR CITIES AND POPULATIONS: Salt Lake City (189,314); West Valley City (132,434); Provo (115,919); West Jordan (108,383); Orem (90,749)

NUMBER OF US CONGRESS MEMBERS: 4 representatives, 2 senators

NUMBER OF ELECTORAL VOTES: 6

NATURAL RESOURCES: coal, natural gas, petroleum, copper, gold, silver, magnesium, salts

AGRICULTURAL PRODUCTS: beef cattle, eggs, greenhouse products, hay, milk

MANUFACTURED GOODS: chemicals, computer products, electronics, metals

STATE HOLIDAYS AND CELEBRATIONS: Pioneer Day, Utah State Fair

GLOSSARY

archaeologist: a scientist who studies bones and tools of ancient people

asphalt: a black substance that is used for making roads

bison: a large North American animal with a big shaggy head, short horns, and a humped back

causeway: a raised road or path that goes across wet ground or water

complex: a group of buildings that are near one another and used for a certain purpose

exhibit: a display that shows something interesting to the public

fossil: ancient remains of plants or animals preserved as rocks

fry bread: a traditional American Indian bread made by deep-frying

lasso: to catch an animal by throwing a rope that has a tied loop on one end

luge: a small sled used for racing down an ice track

mutton: meat of an adult sheep

planetarium: a building or room in which images of stars and planets are shown on a high, curved ceiling

powwow: an American Indian ceremony or social gathering

FURTHER INFORMATION

Graf, Mike. *Arches and Canyonlands National Parks: In the Land of Standing Rocks*. Guilford, CT: FalconGuides, 2013. Read about one family's journey in two of the greatest national parks in the United States.

Kent, Deborah. *Utah*. New York: Scholastic, 2009. Read this introduction to the geography, natural resources, history, economy, important sites, daily life, and people of Utah.

Utah Division of State History
http://ilovehistory.utah.gov
Read about important people and events in Utah's history. Play fun games related to Utah exploration, American Indians, and state maps.

Utah Education Network
http://www.uen.org/counties
Click on an interactive map of Utah counties and learn about what makes each one unique.

Utah Office of Tourism
http://travel.utah.gov/kids
Download photos of Utah for projects, read fast facts, and find out about state symbols, history, and land.

VanVoorst, Jenny Fretland. *What's Great about New Mexico?* Minneapolis: Lerner Publications, 2015. Find out about ten of the most exciting sights in another southwestern state.

INDEX

PHOTO ACKNOWLEDGMENTS

The images in this book are used with the permission of: © Cristina Muraca/Shutterstock Images, p. 1; NASA, pp. 2–3; © Laura Westlund/Independent Picture Service, pp. 4, 27; © Anton Oparin/Shutterstock Images, pp. 4–5, 6–7; © Lauren Orr/Shutterstock Images, p. 5; © Third Cliff Imagery/Alamy, p. 7 (top); © Nata789/Shutterstock Images, p. 7 (bottom); © Steve Estvanik/Shutterstock Images, p. 8; © Robert Johnson/The Standard Examiner/AP Images, pp. 8–9; daveynin/Flickr, p. 9; © Josh Noel/MCT/Newscom, pp. 10, 10–11, 11; PunkToad/Flickr, p. 12; © Andre Jenny Stock Connection Worldwide/Newscom, pp. 12–13; Arthur Bogard, p. 13; © Stephen Saks Photography/Alamy, pp. 14–15, 15 (top); Library of Congress, pp. 15 (bottom) (LC-BH82-4714), 22 (LC-DIG-stereo-1s00827), 29 (bottom right) (LC-DIG-highsm-12003); National Park Service, pp. 16–17; Neal Herbert/National Park Service, p. 17 (top); © Don Land/Shutterstock Images, p. 17 (bottom); Mike Renlund, pp. 18–19; © Douglas C. Pizac/AP Images, p. 19 (top); © Gow27/Shutterstock Images, p. 19 (bottom); © Thinkstock, pp. 20–21, 21 (bottom), 25 (right), 29 (top right); © Universal Images Group Limited/Alamy, p. 21 (top); © Christopher Halloran/Shutterstock Images, pp. 22–23; © Kobby Dagan/Shutterstock Images, p. 23; Jim Moore, pp. 24–25; Kim/Flickr, p. 25 (left); © nicoolay/iStockphoto, p. 26; © Jody Ann/Shutterstock Images, p. 29 (top left); © Alexander Demyanenko/Shutterstock Images, p. 29 (bottom left).

Cover: © Johnny Adolphson/Dreamstime.com, (Arches National Park); Garrett/Wikimedia Commons (CC BY 2.0), (Salt Lake City); © extravagantni/iStock/Thinkstock, (snowboarder); © Laura Westlund/Independent Picture Service (map); © iStockphoto.com/fpm (seal); © iStockphoto.com/vicm (pushpins); © iStockphoto.com/benz190 (cork board).